The 5 W's of Every Old Testament Book

WHO, WHAT, WHEN, WHERE, AND WHY
OF EVERY BOOK IN THE OLD TESTAMENT

Dr. Mike Smith

Franklin Publishing
PRINCETON, TEXAS

Copyright © 2020 by Mike Smith.

All rights reserved. No part of this publication may be reproduced, distributed or transmitted in any form or by any means, including photocopying, recording, or other electronic or mechanical methods, without the prior written permission of the publisher, except in the case of brief quotations embodied in critical reviews and certain other noncommercial uses permitted by copyright law. For permission requests, write to the publisher, addressed "Attention: Permissions Coordinator," at the address below.

Kelly Carr / Franklin Publishing
1215 Juniper
Princeton, Texas 75407

www.FranklinPublishing.org

Ordering Information:

Quantity sales. Special discounts are available on quantity purchases by corporations, associations, and others. For details, contact the "Special Sales Department" at the address above.

Except where otherwise indicated, all Scripture quotations are taken from the New King James Version®. Copyright © 1982 by Thomas Nelson. Used by permission. All rights reserved.

The 5 W's of Every Old Testament Book: Who, What, When, Where, and Why of Every Book in the Old Testament / Mike Smith. —1st ed.

Copyright © 2020 by Franklin Publishing

Printed in the United States of America by Franklin Publishing, 2020

All rights reserved.
ISBN-13: 978-1-7320028-6-9
ISBN-10: 1-7320028-6-X

Dedication

I have been blessed to sit under some great, Godly teachers of the Bible. Several have had an influence on my life, but I was so young that I cannot recall their names. I do know they made Sunday School fun and I had a desire to attend. My parents never left me crying or had to force me to go. I think God for those unnamed, unsung heroes. I thank Evelyn Bell for teaching youth at FBC Bellville, TX and for her husband, Alvis Bell, who was my pastor. He was a very Godly man who, along with Charles Murphy, also went the extra mile to teach me in Royal Ambassadors. I thank God for them.

I thank my parents, L.C. and Dot Smith, who were not trained but were willing to teach the youth Sunday evening Training Union class so we would have a teacher. I thank God for them and all the willing workers who served but were not necessarily gifted or called.

I thank the college and seminary professors I sat under. They were model teachers and personal encouragers in my life. Men such as Dr. Ray Summers, Dr. Huber Drumwright, Dr. Roy Fish, Dr. Jack Terry, and others I know I am leaving out. They were educated and created a desire for me to learn.

I thank pastors and evangelist friends who were extraordinary teachers of the Bible that I had the privilege of sitting under, like Dr Adrian Rogers, Dr Warren Wiersbe, Dr. Jerry Vines, Dr. Bob Pittman, Dr. Herb Reavis, Art Fineout, Dr. D. L. Lowrie, and

Herman Cramer. These men were gifted in making the Bible come alive. I thank God for them.

One last Bible teacher I must acknowledge that has had a lasting impact on my life is Kenneth Simmons. He was an uneducated East Texas roughneck that God called to preach. He, without reservation, was the best home Bible study teacher that I ever sat under. I was his pastor for three years his friend until God called him home.

I love studying the Word and having the Holy Spirit teach me so I can teach others.

So, I dedicate this book to all who teach the Word.

Contents

Introduction 11

1 Overview of the Bible 13

   Section 1: THE LAW 17

2 Genesis 5 W's 18

3 Exodus 5 W's 22

4 Leviticus 5 W's 25

5 Numbers 5 W's 28

6 Deuteronomy 5 W's 30

   Section 2: HISTORY 33

7 Joshua 5 W's 34

8 Judges 5 W's 37

9 Ruth 5 W's 39

10 1 & 2 Samuel 5 W's 41

11 1 & 2 Kings 5 W's 43

12 1 & 2 Chronicles 5 W's 45

13 Ezra 5 W's 47

14 Nehemiah 5 W's 49

15 Esther 5 W's 51

   Section 3: POETRY 53

Chapter 16	Job 5 W's	54
Chapter 17	Psalms 5 W's	56
Chapter 18	Proverbs 5 W's	58
Chapter 19	Ecclesiastes 5 W's	60
Chapter 20	Song of Solomon 5 W's	62
Section 4: MAJOR PROPHETS		65
Chapter 21	Isaiah 5 W's	66
Chapter 22	Jeremiah 5 W's	70
Chapter 23	Lamentations 5 W's	72
Chapter 24	Ezekiel 5 W's	74
Chapter 25	Daniel 5 W's	76
Section 5: MINOR PROPHETS		79
Chapter 26	Hosea 5 W's	80
Chapter 27	Joel 5 W's	82
Chapter 28	Amos 5 W's	84
Chapter 29	Obadiah 5 W's	86
Chapter 30	Jonah 5 W's	88
Chapter 31	Micah 5 W's	90
Chapter 32	Nahum 5 W's	92
Chapter 33	Habakkuk 5 W's	94
Chapter 34	Zephaniah 5 W's	96
Chapter 35	Haggai 5 W's	98
Chapter 36	Zechariah 5 W's	100
Chapter 37	Malachi 5 W's	102

Bibliography	105
ABOUT THE AUTHOR	107

INTRODUCTION

The Who-What-When-Where-Why of the Old Testament is a survey of the basic facts of the Old Testament. Before anyone can properly interpret the message of a biblical passage, a knowledge of the background of that book is essential. This book provides that basic background knowledge.

The books are designed for college freshmen taking an Old Testament 1301 survey course. It also can be helpful for any Bible study leader or student. The material, such as dates, does not try to pinpoint or discuss various views, but simply rounds off a date to make it easier to retain. The book does not enter into deep discussion of various possible authors, but simply selects the most conservative choice. The desire is to provide a quick, simple resource that will stimulate future deeper study of the Bible. The format is that of PowerPoint slides. This book is not a narrative, but quick snapshots of essential background study material.

1

Overview of the Bible

Before we look at Genesis, let's review the outline of the 66 books of the Bible.

There are two major divisions:
- Old Testament – 39 books
- New Testament – 27 books
- Total – 66 books

OLD TESTAMENT DIVISION
- Law – 5 books
- History – 12 books
- Poetry – 5 books
- Major Prophets – 5 books
- Minor Prophets – 12 books
- Total – 39 books

Every book in the Old Testament will fall into one of these divisions. This answers the question of what kind of book it is.

NEW TESTAMENT DIVISION

- Gospels – 4 books
- History – 1 book
- Letters from Paul – 13 books
- Letters from Others – 8 books
- Prophecy – 1 book
- Total – 27 books

THE FIRST FIVE BOOKS OF THE OLD TESTAMENT

Pentateuch, Law, Torah, Books of Moses. Why these titles?

1. Pentateuch
- The word "Pentateuch" comes from the Greek word "pente," which means "five."
- The Pentateuch is God's instruction for a nation learning to be God's people in this world.
- The Pentateuch has:
  - i) Stories
  - ii) Laws (the laws give us boundaries for our lives). [1]
2. Law

---

[1] Wilkinson

- "Law" is common expression for the first five books of the Bible. "Law" is also used to refer to the Ten Commandments.
3. Torah
- The Hebrew word "Torah" is used to refer to the Law. The root word of Torah means "direction" or "teaching."
4. Books of Moses
- The "Books of Moses" is also used for the first five books, for he was the human author.

FORMAT

- For every book, we will use this outline:

5 W's
    i) Who
    ii) What
    iii) When
    iv) Where
    v) Why
        (1) Key Word
        (2) Key Verse
        (3) Key to See Jesus

5 W's
- Five basic facts are used to answer basic questions about each book:
    i) Who? – Who is the human author God used to write the book?
    ii) What? – What division of the Bible does this book belong to?
    iii) When? – What was the date when the book was written?

iv) Where? – Where was the book written from?

v) Why? – Why was it written? We will identify a key word, a key verse, and point out a key to see Jesus in the book.

- Every Bible student should seek to learn these 5 W's for each book of the Bible as a foundation for deeper study.

Section 1:
THE LAW

2

Genesis 5 W's

WHO WROTE GENESIS? MOSES

a. Testimony from the Old Testament:

Exodus 17:14; 24:4, "And the LORD said unto Moses, Write this for a memorial in a book, and rehearse it in the ears of Joshua: for I will utterly put out the remembrance of Amalek from under heaven...And Moses wrote all the words of the LORD, and rose up early in the morning, and built an altar under the hill, and twelve pillars, according to the twelve tribes of Israel."

Daniel 9:11, "...the oath that is written in the law of Moses the servant of God..."

b. Testimony from the New Testament:

John 5:46, "For had ye believed Moses, ye would have believed me; for he wrote of me."

John 7:19, "Did not Moses give you the law...?"

Acts 26:22, "...which the prophets and Moses did say should come..."

Romans 10:19, "First Moses saith, I will provoke you to jealousy by them that are no people, and by a foolish nation I will anger you (Deuteronomy 32:21)."
  a. Some say Moses could not have written Genesis because:
     i. It records his death.
     ii. It uses names that do not fit the time.
     iii. It talks about Moses' humility.
  b. HOW COULD MOSES WRITE GENESIS? The answer is the Holy Spirit.

WHAT IS GENESIS? LAW

  c. The Old Testament's literature can be distinguished as:
     i. Law
     ii. History
     iii. Poetry
     iv. Prophecy
  a. Genesis is a part of literature we call "The Law."
  b. The Hebrew title is *"Bereshit,"* from the first word in the book meaning "in the beginning."
  c. The name "Genesis" from the Greek word *"gignesthai,"* which means "beginnings" and "to be born."
  d. Genesis is LAW.

WHEN DID GENESIS TAKE PLACE? 1400 B.C.

  a. Timeline of events in Genesis

      i. Creation – 4000 B.C.
     ii. Death of Abraham – 2000 B.C.
    iii. Joseph in Egypt – 1900 B.C.
    iv. Death of Joseph – 1800 B.C.
     v. Date of Exodus – 1500-1400 B.C.
    vi. Death of Moses – 1400 B.C.[2]

b. Genesis was probably written during the 40-year wandering from 1440-1400 B.C.
      i. To round off, we use the date as 1400 B.C.

c. Dates are rounded off to make them easier to remember.[3]

d. Genesis was written about 1400 B.C.

WHERE DID GENESIS TAKE PLACE? WILDERNESS WANDERING

a. The events in Genesis took place in three primary places:
      i. The Garden of Eden probably located in present-day Iraq.
     ii. Abraham starts out from Ur in Iraq and goes north to Haram then to Israel.
    iii. The book concludes with Joseph's family in northern Egypt.

b. Moses probably wrote the book while wandering in the wilderness (Sinai Desert).

WHY WAS GENESIS WRITTEN?

a. The KEY WORD in Genesis is Beginnings.
      i. Beginning of the world – Genesis 1

---

[2] Willmington's, p. xx-xxi
[3] Willmington's, p. xx-xxi

ii. Beginning of human race – Genesis 2
  iii. Beginning of sin – Genesis 3
  iv. Beginning of redemption – Genesis 3
  v. Beginning of Hebrew nation – Genesis 12-50
 b. The KEY VERSE in Genesis is Genesis 1:1 "In the beginning God created the Heaven and the earth."
 c. The KEYS TO SEE JESUS in Genesis are:
  i. Jesus is Creator
  ii. Jesus is the seed of a woman
  iii. Jesus is Abraham's Lamb.

Genesis 3:15, "And I will put enmity between thee and the woman, and between thy seed and her seed; it shall bruise thy head, and thou shalt bruise his heel."[4]

---

[4] Wilkinson and Boa, p. 8

3

Exodus 5 W's

WHO WROTE EXODUS? MOSES

a. External Evidence

- Joshua 8:30-32; Malachi 4:4; John 1:45; Romans 10:5; Mark 7:10; 12:26; Luke 20:37; John 5:46-47

John 1:45, "Phillip findeth Nathaniel, and saith unto him, we have found him, of whom Moses in the law, and the prophets, did write, Jesus of Nazareth, the son of Joseph.

Mark 7:10, "For Moses said, Honour thy father and thy mother; and whoso curseth father or mother, let him die the death..."

b. Internal Evidence

- Exodus 15; 17:8-14; 20:1-17; 24:7, 12

Exodus 24:4, "And Moses wrote all the words of the LORD, and rose up early in the morning, and builded an altar under the hill, and twelve pillars, according to the twelve tribes of Israel."

WHAT IS EXODUS? LAW

a. Genesis, Exodus, Leviticus, Numbers, and Deuteronomy are referred to as the Law, Books of Moses, Torah, and Pentateuch.

- The Hebrew word is *"we'elleh shemeth"* from Exodus 1:1, "Now these are the names..."[5]
- The Greek word is "Exodus" meaning "exit", "departure," or "going out."

b. Exodus refers to Israel going out of Egypt.

WHEN DID EXODUS TAKE PLACE? 1400 B.C.

a. During the wilderness wandering

b. Exodus covers the time from arrival of Jacob in Egypt in 1800 B.C. to the erection of the tabernacle in 1400 B.C. [6]

WHERE DID EXODUS TAKE PLACE? WILDERNESS WANDERING

a. Egypt and Canaan

- Exodus 1-13 – Egypt for 430 years [7]
- Exodus 13-18 – Wilderness

---

[5] Biblehub.com/interlinear/exodus/1.htm
[6] Rose, p.1
[7] Rose, p.1

- Exodus 19-40 – Mount Sinai

b. Exodus was written during the wilderness wandering in the Sinai Desert.

WHY WAS EXODUS WRITTEN? REDEMPTION

a. KEY WORD – Redemption
- Redemption as seen in the Passover
- Deliverance as seen in the Exodus

b. KEY VERSE—Exodus 6:6

"Wherefore say unto the children of Israel, I am the LORD, and I will bring you out from under the burdens of the Egyptians, and I will rid you out of their bondage, and I will redeem you with a stretched out arm, and with great judgments."

c. KEY TO SEE JESUS– Jesus in Exodus is our Passover Lamb[8]

---

[8] Wilkinson and Boa, p. 14

4

Leviticus 5 W's

WHO WROTE LEVITICUS? MOSES

Leviticus 1:1, "And the LORD called unto Moses, and spake unto him out of the tabernacle of the congregation, saying..."

Leviticus 4:1, "And the LORD spake unto Moses, saying..."

Leviticus 6:1, "And the LORD spake unto Moses, saying..."

Leviticus 8:1, "And the LORD spake unto Moses, saying..."

WHAT IS LEVITICUS? LAW

a. The Hebrew word is "*wayyigra*", the first word of the text. [9]

---

[9] (Biblehub.com/interlinear/Leviticus/1.htm)

b. The Greek word is "Leviticus"; in the Septuagint, *"leutikon"* means "that which pertains to the priest."

c. Some say Leviticus is a priest's manual. Today, we have pastor's manuals on how to do weddings and funerals. Leviticus was the priest's manual on how to be a priest. [10]

WHEN DID LEVITICUS TAKE PLACE? 1400 B.C.

a. During a one-month period in 1400 B.C. during the wilderness wandering in the Sinai Desert [11]

WHERE DID LEVITICUS TAKE PLACE? WILDERNESS WANDERING

WHY WAS LEVITICUS WRITTEN?

a. KEY WORDS

- Holy – used 90 times, used 152 times in all forms
- Sanctify – used 17 times

b. KEY VERSE— Leviticus 11:44-45

"For I am the LORD your God: ye shall therefore sanctify yourselves, and ye shall be holy; for I am holy; neither shall ye defile yourselves with any manner of creeping thing that creepeth upon the earth. For I am the LORD that bringeth you up out

---

[10] Rose, p.1
[11] Rose, p.1

of the land of Egypt, to be your God: ye shall therefore be holy, for I am holy."

    c. KEY TO SEE JESUS—In Leviticus, Jesus is the Holy One, our High Priest. [12]

---

[12] Willmington, p. 22

5

Numbers 5 W's

WHO WROTE NUMBERS? MOSES

Numbers 1:1, "And the LORD spake unto Moses in the wilderness of Sinai, in the tabernacle of the congregation, on the first day of the second month, in the second year after they were come out of the land of Egypt, saying...."

WHAT IS NUMBERS? LAW

a. The Hebrew word is *"bemidbar"* meaning "in the wilderness."[13]
b. The Greek word in the Septuagint is *"arithmoi"* meaning "numbers."
c. The Latin Vulgate says *"liber numeri"* meaning "book of numbers.[14]

---

[13] Biblehub.com/interlinear/numbers/1.htm
[14] Rose, p. 1

WHEN DID NUMBERS TAKE PLACE? 1,400 B.C.

a. Numbers covers a period of 40 years: 1440-1400 B.C.[15]

WHERE DID NUMBERS TAKE PLACE? WILDERNESS WANDERING

WHY WAS NUMBERS WRITTEN?

a. KEY WORD—WANDERINGS[16]

b. KEY VERSE—Numbers 6:24-26

"The LORD bless thee, and keep thee: The LORD make his face shine upon thee and be gracious unto thee: The LORD lift up his countenance upon thee and give thee peace."

c. KEY TO SEE JESUS—Jesus is our Deliverer.

---

[15] Rose, p. 1
[16] Willmington's, p. 29

6

Deuteronomy 5 W's

WHO WROTE DEUTERONOMY? MOSES

    a. 40 times Deuteronomy states that Moses is the author:

e.g., Deuteronomy 1:1, "These be the words which Moses spake unto all Israel on this side Jordan in the wilderness, in the plain over against the Red Sea, between Paran, and Tophel, and Laban, and Hazeroth, and Dizahab."

    b. Jesus attributes the book to Moses:

Matthew 19:7-9, "They say unto him, why did Moses then command to give a writing of divorcement, and to put her away? He saith unto them, Moses because of the hardness of your hearts suffered you to put away your wives: but from the beginning it was not so. And I say unto you, whosoever shall put away his wife, except it be for fornication, and shall marry another, committeth adultery: and whose marrieth her which is put away doth commit adultery.

John 5:45-47, "Do not think that I will accuse you to the Father. There is one who accuses you: Moses, on whom you have set your hope. For if you believed Moses, you would believe me; for he wrote of me. But if you do not believe his writings, how will you believe my words?"

WHAT IS DEUTERONOMY? LAW

a. The word comes from the Greek "*deuteronomion*" meaning "second law" from Deut. 17:18 [17]

b. This is not a second law but a copy of the law.

WHEN DID DEUTERONOMY TAKE PLACE? 1,400 B.C.

a. Covers a period of about a month in 1400 B.C.

WHERE DID DEUTERONOMY TAKE PLACE? WILDERNESS WANDERING

a. In the Sinai desert
b. On the plains of Moab due east of Jericho and the Jordan River and at the end of the 40 years of wandering

WHY WAS DEUTERONOMY WRITTEN?

a. KEY WORD—Second Law

---

[17] Rose Bible Overview, p. 35

b. KEY VERSE—Deuteronomy 10:12-13

"And now, Israel, what doth the LORD thy God require of thee, but to fear the LORD thy God, to walk in all his ways, and to love him, and to serve the LORD thy God with all thy heart and with all thy soul, To keep the commandments of the LORD, and his statutes, which I command thee this day for thy good?"

c. KEY TO SEE JESUS

Moses is a type of Christ, for he is the only other to fill the same three offices as Christ did: Prophet, Priest and King. [18]

---

[18] Wilkinson and Boa, p. 38-39

Section 2: HISTORY

7

Joshua 5 W's

WHO WROTE JOSHUA? JOSHUA

a. Joshua 24:16, "Then Joshua wrote these words…"
b. Short biography:
   - He was born a slave in Egypt.
   - He was Moses' leader of the army and became his successor to conquer the Promised Land.
   - He had faith, courage, and dedication to God.[19]
c. Joshua's name was "*Hoshea*," meaning "salvation" (Numbers 13:8).
   - Moses changed Joshua's name to "*Jehoshua*," meaning "salvation" (Numbers 13:16).

---

[19] Hanke, p. 149

- When the spies came back, Jehoshua became Joshua (Numbers 14:6).
- The Greek name is "*Iesous*," or "Jesus." [20]

WHAT IS JOSHUA? HISTORY

a. Joshua is part of **12 historical books** that deal with the history of Israel.

WHEN DID JOSHUA TAKE PLACE? 1,300 B.C.

a. 1400 B.C. – Death of Moses
b. 1300 B.C. – Death of Joshua

WHERE DID JOSHUA TAKE PLACE? CANAAN

a. The book is divided into 3 geographical settings:
  - The Jordan River – Chapters 1-5
  - Canaan – Chapters 6-13
  - The 12 Tribes – Chapters 13-24

WHY WAS JOSHUA WRITTEN?

a. KEY WORD—CONQUEST
  - Historically, Joshua shows the conquering of the land of Israel.
  - Theologically, Joshua teaches that victory and blessing come through obedience and trust in God.
b. KEY VERSE— Joshua 1:6-9

---

[20] Hanke, p. 149

"Be strong and of a good courage: for unto this people shalt thou divide for an inheritance the land, which I sware unto their fathers to give them. Only be thou strong and very courageous, that thou mayest observe to do according to all the law, which Moses my servant commanded thee: turn not from it to the right hand or to the left, that thou mayest prosper withersoever thou goest. This book of the law shall not depart out of thy mouth; but thou shalt meditate therein day and night, that thou mayest observe to do according to all that is written therein: for then thou shalt make thy way prosperous, and then thou shall have good success. Have not I commanded thee? Be strong and of a good courage; be not afraid, neither by thou dismayed: for the LORD thy God is with thee whithersoever thou goest."

    c. KEY TO SEE JESUS—Jesus is the Captain of the Lord's host.

8

Judges 5 W's

WHO WROTE JUDGES? SAMUEL

a. The Author is unknown, but it was probably Samuel.
b. Therefore, we say Samuel.

WHAT IS JUDGES? HISTORY

a. Judges is a historical book, named after the judges who ruled Israel.
b. Judges is contrasted with the book of Joshua. In Joshua, the people were obedient and victorious; in Judges, the people were disobedient and suffered defeat.

WHEN DID JUDGES TAKE PLACE?
1,000 B.C.

WHERE DID JUDGES TAKE PLACE?
CANAAN

WHY WAS JUDGES WRITTEN?

a. KEY WORD—CYCLES
- To record the history of Israel from the time of Samuel to the beginning of the United Kingdom is time in repeated cycles. Israel would get away from God. God would send an enemy nation to invade Israel. Israel would cry to God for help. God would raise up a judge to deliver Israel. Then we see same cycle repeated.
- Judges 21:25, "In those days there was no king in Israel: every man did that which was right in his own eyes."

b. KEY VERSE—Judges 21:25

"In those days there was no king in Israel: every man did that which was right in his own eyes."

c. KEY TO SEE JESUS—JESUS IS OUR DELIVERER.

9

Ruth 5 W's

WHO WROTE RUTH? RUTH

a. Talmudic tradition says Samuel wrote the book of Ruth, but this is unlikely since David appears in Ruth 4:17, 22, and Samuel died before David was made king.
b. Ruth could have written this book. [21]

WHAT IS RUTH? HISTORY

a. The Hebrew title of the book means "friendship."[22]

WHEN DID RUTH TAKE PLACE? 1,000 B.C.

a. During the time of the judges.

---

[21] Wilkinson and Boa, p. 66
[22] Wilkinson and Boa, p. 66

WHERE DID RUTH TAKE PLACE? BETHLEHEM

a. 4 Distinct Settings:
- Moab (1:1-18) ten years
- Bethlehem (1:19-2:23) several months
- Threshing floor in Bethlehem (chapter 3) one day
- City of Bethlehem (chapter 4) one year[23]

WHY WAS RUTH WRITTEN?

a. KEY WORD—KINSMAN-REDEEMER
- Ruth is a love story that presents a positive picture of faith and obedience and godliness.
- The theme is redemption.

b. KEY VERSE—Ruth 1:16

"And Ruth said, Intreat me not to leave thee, or to return from following after thee: for whither thou goest, I will go; and where thou lodgest, I will lodge: thy people shall be my people, and thy God my God..."

c. KEY TO SEE JESUS—Jesus is our Kinsman-Redeemer.

---

[23] Wilkinson and Boa, P. 99

10

1 & 2 Samuel 5 W's

WHO WROTE 1 & 2 SAMUEL? SAMUEL

a. Some say that the author is unknown.
b. "Samuel" means "the name of God" or "heard of God."

WHAT IS 1 & 2 SAMUEL? HISTORY

a. 1 and 2 Samuel are historical books.
b. 1 & 2 Samuel were one book in the Hebrew Bible.

WHEN DID 1 & 2 SAMUEL TAKE PLACE? 1100 B.C.[24]

WHERE DID 1 & 2 SAMUEL TAKE PLACE? CANAAN

a. Primarily in Jerusalem

---

[24] Rose Chart, p. 2

WHY WAS 1 & 2 SAMUEL WRITTEN?

    a. KEY WORD— TRANSITION
- To record the history of Israel's early kings

    b. KEY VERSES

1 Samuel 17:45, "Then said David to the Philistine, Thou comest to me with a sword, and with a spear, and with a shield: but I come to thee in the name of the LORD of hosts, the God of the armies of Israel, whom thou hast defied."

2 Samuel 7:9, "And I was with thee whithersoever thou wentest, and have cut off all thine enemies out of thy sight, and have made thee a great name, like unto the name of the great men that are in the earth."

    c. KEYS TO SEE JESUS
- 1 Samuel – Prophet, Priest, and King
- 2 Samuel – Sweet singer of Israel

11

1 & 2 Kings 5 W's

WHO WROTE 1 & 2 KINGS? JEREMIAH

WHAT IS 1 & 2 KINGS? HISTORY

a. Historical books
b. 1 & 2 Kings were one book in the Hebrew Bible
c. Named after kings of Israel

WHEN DID 1 & 2 KINGS TAKE PLACE? 500 B.C.[25]

WHERE DID 1 & 2 KINGS TAKE PLACE? CANAAN AND ISRAEL

a. In Israel before and after the captivity.

---

[25] Rose Chart, p. 3

WHY WAS 1 & 2 KINGS WRITTEN?

a. KEY WORD—DIVISION
- Division of The Kingdom
- Captivity

b. KEY VERSE—1 Kings 3:10-13

"And the speech pleased the Lord, that Solomon had asked this thing. And God said unto him, Because thou hast asked this thing, and hast not asked for thyself long life; neither hast asked riches for thyself, nor hast asked for the life of thine enemies; but hast asked for thyself understanding to discern judgment; Behold, I have done according to thy words: lo, I have given thee a wise and an understanding heart; so that there was none like thee before thee, neither after thee shall any arise like unto thee. And I have also given thee that which thou hast not asked, both riches, and honour: so that there shall not be any among the kings like unto thee all thy days."

c. KEYS TO SEE JESUS
- 1 Kings – Our Ruler
- 2 Kings – Powerful Prophet

12

1 & 2 Chronicles 5 W's

WHO WROTE 1 & 2 CHRONICLES? EZRA [26]

WHAT IS 1 & 2 CHRONICLES? HISTORY

a. Historical books
b. 1 & 2 Chronicles were one book in the Hebrew Bible

WHEN DID 1 & 2 CHRONICLES TAKE PLACE? 400 B.C.[27]

WHERE DID 1 & 2 CHRONICLES TAKE PLACE? ISRAEL

a. In Israel before and after the captivity

---

[26] Rose Chart, p. 3
[27] Rose Chart, p. 3

WHY WAS 1 & 2 CHRONICLES WRITTEN?

   a. KEY WORD—DAVIDIC COVENANT
- To present a spiritual perspective to the history
- To give encouragement to the remnant [28]

   b. KEY VERSE—2 Chronicles 7:14

"If my people, which are called by my name, shall humble themselves, and pray, and seek my face, and turn from their wicked ways; then will I hear from heaven, and will forgive their sin, and will heal their land."

   c. KEYS TO SEE JESUS
- 1 Chronicles – Son of David
- 2 Chronicles – Jesus is the Temple

---

[28] Rose Chart, p. 3

13

Ezra 5 W's

WHO WROTE EZRA? EZRA

a. Jewish tradition holds that Ezra the priest wrote Ezra-Nehemiah.
b. In Ezra 7:6, 28-9:15, the first person "I", "me", and "my" is used.[29]
c. Ezra is the Aramaic form of the Hebrew word "*ezer*" meaning "help" or "God's help."[30]

WHAT IS EZRA? HISTORY

a. Historical book

---

[29] Ultimate Bible Guide, p. 132
[30] Wilkinson and Boa, p. 117

WHEN DID EZRA TAKE PLACE?
400 B.C.[31]

WHERE DID EZRA TAKE PLACE?
BABYLON & JERUSALEM

a. Captivity in Babylon and in Jerusalem
b. Zerubbabel led the first group back to Jerusalem in 538 B.C.
c. Ezra led 2nd group bac 457 B.C.
d. Nehemiah led 3rd group back to Jerusalem in 444 B.C

WHY WAS EZRA WRITTEN?

a. KEY WORD—RESTORATION
- The theme is spiritual and moral restoration under leadership of Zerubbabel and Ezra.

b. KEY VERSE—Ezra 7:8-10

"And he came to Jerusalem in the fifth month, which was in the seventh year of the king. For upon the first day of the first month began he to go up from Babylon, and on the first day of the fifth month came he to Jerusalem, according to the good hand of his God upon him. For Ezra had prepared his heart to seek the law of the LORD, and to do it, and to teach in Israel statues and judgments."

c. KEY TO SEE JESUS—He is the Restorer of the Temple.

---

[31] Rose, p. 3

14

Nehemiah 5 W's

WHO WROTE NEHEMIAH? NEHEMIAH

a. Some think Ezra wrote the book, but Nehemiah 1:1 says "the words of Nehemiah."[32]

WHAT IS NEHEMIAH? HISTORY

a. Historical Book

WHEN DID NEHEMIAH TAKE PLACE? 400 B.C.

WHERE DID NEHEMIAH TAKE PLACE? BABYLON & JERUSALEM

a. Captivity in Babylon
b. Return to Jerusalem

---

[32] Wilkinson and Boa, p. 124

WHY WAS NEHEMIAH WRITTEN?

a. KEY WORD—RESTORATION OF WALL
- Ezra dealt with the religious restoration.
- Nehemiah deals with the political restoration.
- Zerubbabel restored the Temple.
- Ezra restored the temple sacrifices and the priestly order.
- Nehemiah restored the wall.[33]

b. KEY VERSE—Nehemiah 1:5

"And said, I beseech thee, O LORD God of heaven, the great and terrible God, that keepeth covenant and mercy for them that love him and observe his commandments..."

c. KEY TO SEE JESUS—Jesus is the Restorer of the Nation.

---

[33] Wilkerson, p. 125

15

Esther 5 W's

WHO WROTE ESTHER? MORDECAI

WHAT IS ESTHER? HISTORY

a. Historical book
b. Esther's name is Hebrew meaning to hide or conceal.
c. Her additional name, "*Hadassah*," means "myrtle"[34]

WHEN DID ESTHER TAKE PLACE? 400 B.C.

WHERE DID ESTHER TAKE PLACE? SUSA, PERSIA

a. The palace at Susa, Persia

---

[34] Wilkerson, p. 131

WHY WAS ESTHER WRITTEN?

a. KEY WORD—PROVIDENCE
- Esther deals with the protection and preservation of God's people.

b. KEY VERSE—Esther 4:14

"For if thou altogether holdest thy peace at this time, then shall there enlargement and deliverance arise to the Jews from another place; but thou and thy father's house shall be destroyed: and who knoweth whether thou art come to the kingdom for such a time as this?"

c. KEY TO SEE JESUS—Jesus is our Advocate.[35]

---

[35] Wilkerson, p. 132

Section 3: POETRY

Chapter 16

Job 5 W's

WHO WROTE JOB? MOSES

a. Unknown, could be Job or Moses.
b. "*Iyyob*" is the Hebrew title and means "persecuted one," or the Arabic word means "to repent."
c. Job took place before the Wilderness Wandering. Moses probably was told the story in oral form and he writes it under Gods inspiration.

WHAT IS JOB? WISDOM

a. Part of poetic literature, also called wisdom literature
b. Job is perhaps the oldest book in the Bible.
c. The book tells of a man who lost everything and wrestles with the question, "Why?"[36]

---

[36] Wilkerson, p. 144

WHEN DID JOB TAKE PLACE? 1,400 B.C.

a. During the Patriarchal period, written around 1400 B.C. during the wilderness wandering in the Sinai Desert
b. It is the oldest book chronologically in the Bible

WHERE DID JOB TAKE PLACE? WILDERNESS WANDERING

a. Job 4:21 locates Uz in the area of Edom, southeast of the Dead Sea.
b. Uz is adjacent to Midian where Moses lived for 40 years.[37]

WHY WAS JOB WRITTEN?

a. KEY WORD—SOVEREIGNTY
   - The basic question: Why do the righteous suffer if God is loving and all-powerful?
   - Conclusion: God is sovereign and worthy of worship in whatever He chooses to do. Job learned to trust God.[38]
b. KEY VERSE—Job 13:15
"Though he slay me, yet will I trust in him..."
c. KEY TO SEE JESUS—Jesus is Patience, the Ancient of Days.

---

[37] Wilkerson, p. 144
[38] Wilkerson, p. 150

Chapter 17

Psalms 5 W's

WHO WROTE PSALMS? DAVID

a. David – 75 psalms
b. Asaph, a priest or music director – 12 psalms
c. Sons of Korah, singers – 10 psalms
d. Solomon – 2 psalms
e. Moses – 1 psalm
f. Heman, a wise man – 1 psalm
g. Ethan, a wise man – 1 psalm
h. Anonymous, some may be by Ezra – 50 psalms[39]

WHAT IS PSALMS?   WISDOM

a. Poetry/wisdom literature

---

[39] Hanke, p. 199

b. "Psalms" is from the Greek word meaning, "A song sung to the accompaniment of a plucked instrument."[40]

WHEN DID PSALMS TAKE PLACE?
1,000 B.C.

a. Covers a wide span of time from Moses (1400 B.C.) to Ezra (400 B.C.).
b. The Davidic Psalms written 1000 B.C.[41]

WHERE DID PSALMS TAKE PLACE?
JERUSALEM

a. Wide range of places; depends on the author
b. Davidic Psalms were written in Jerusalem.[42]

WHY WAS PSALMS WRITTEN?

a. KEY WORD—WORSHIP
   - The basic theme is worship.
   - It is a hymn book, a song book to praise God.
b. KEY VERSE—Psalm 19:14

"Let the words of my mouth, and the meditation of my heart, be acceptable in thy sight, O LORD, my strength, and my redeemer."

c. KEY TO SEE JESUS—Jesus is my Shepherd

---

[40] Wilkinson and Boa, p. 152
[41] Rose, p. 4
[42] Wilkinson and Boa, p. 153

Chapter 18

Proverbs 5 W's

WHO WROTE PROVERBS? SOLOMON

a. 1 Kings 4:32 says he spoke more than 3,000 proverbs and 1,005 songs.
b. In our book, we only have 800 proverbs.[43]
c. There are other writers, but we accept Solomon as the editor of all the proverbs.

WHAT IS PROVERBS? WISDOM

a. Part of wisdom literature
b. The Hebrew title is "*mishle shelomob*," meaning "Proverbs of Solomon."
c. "Pro" means "for", and "*verba*" means "words"[44]

---

[43] Wilkinson and Boa, p. 162
[44] Ultimate Bible Guide, p. 169

WHEN DID PROVERBS TAKE PLACE? 900 B.C.

a. Solomon wrote Song of Solomon as a young man – 970 B.C.
b. Solomon wrote Proverbs as a middle-aged man – 950 B.C.
c. Solomon wrote Ecclesiastes as an old man – 930 B.C.[45]

WHERE DID PROVERBS TAKE PLACE? JERUSALEM

a. Probably Jerusalem

WHY WAS PROVERBS WRITTEN?

a. KEY WORD—WISDOM
   - To promote discernment and wise living
   - Proverbs is difficult to outline, because the subjects jump around.
b. KEY VERSE—Proverbs 3:5-6

"Trust in the LORD with all thine heart; and lean not unto thine own understanding. In all thy ways acknowledge him, and he shall direct thy paths."

c. KEY TO SEE JESUS—Jesus is Wisdom.

---

[45] Rose, p. 4

Chapter 19

Ecclesiastes 5 W's

WHO WROTE ECCLESIASTES? SOLOMON

WHAT IS ECCLESIASTES? WISDOM

a. Wisdom literature
b. The Hebrew title is "*Qoheleth*," which is a rare term only in Ecclesiastes in the Old Testament. It comes from the word "*Qahal*,", meaning "to call for assembly" or "one who addresses an assembly," or "preacher."[46]

WHEN DID ECCLESIASTES TAKE PLACE? 900 B.C.

a. 930-900 B.C., late in Solomon's life[47]

---

[46] Wilkinson and Boa, p. 169
[47] Wilkinson and Boa, p. 169

WHERE DID ECCLESIASTES TAKE PLACE? JERUSALEM[48]

WHY WAS ECCLESIASTES WRITTEN?

a. KEY WORD—VANITY
  - To show that the only meaning in life is God.
b. KEY VERSE—Ecclesiastes 1:2
"Vanity of vanities, saith the Preacher, vanity of vanities; all is vanity."
c. KEY TO SEE JESUS—Jesus is the Preacher.

---

[48] Rose, p. 4

Chapter 20

Song of Solomon 5 W's

WHO WROTE SONG OF SOLOMON? SOLOMON

WHAT IS SONG OF SOLOMON? WISDOM

a. Part of wisdom literature
b. Comes from Song of Solomon 1:1 – it is a love story.

WHEN DID SONG OF SOLOMON TAKE PLACE? 900 B.C.

a. 970-900 B.C., early in Solomon's life[49]

---

[49] Wilkinson and Boa, p. 177

WHERE DID SONG OF SOLOMON TAKE PLACE? JERUSALEM

WHY WAS SONG OF SOLOMON WRITTEN?

   a. KEY WORD—LOVE
- A love story that shows God's love for His people

   b. KEY VERSE—Song of Solomon 2:2-4

"As the lily among thorns, so is my love among the daughters. As the apple tree among the trees of the wood, so is my beloved among the sons. I sat down under his shadow with great delight, and his fruit was sweet to my taste. He brought me to the banqueting house, and his banner over me was love."

   c. KEY TO SEE JESUS—Jesus is the Rose of Sharon and the Lily of the Valley.

Section 4: MAJOR PROPHETS

Chapter 21

Isaiah 5 W's

WHO WROTE ISAIAH? ISAIAH

a. "Isaiah" means "Yahweh is Salvation."

WHAT IS ISAIAH?   MAJOR PROPHET

a. Isaiah is a part of the literature called the prophets.
b. Isaiah is the first of 17 prophetical books
   - There are five major prophetic books in the Bible:
     1. Isaiah
     2. Jeremiah
     3. Lamentations
     4. Ezekiel
     5. Daniel
   - There are 12 minor prophetic books in the Bible:
     1. Hosea
     2. Joel

3. Amos
4. Obadiah
5. Jonah
6. Micah
7. Nahum
8. Habakkuk
9. Zephaniah
10. Haggai
11. Zechariah
12. Malachi

c. What is the difference between a major prophet and a minor prophet?
   - Length of book
   - It has nothing to do with value or importance.
d. Prophets were called prophets, seers, watchmen, and men of God.
   - A prophet was one who spoke for God.
   - The word "prophet" is used over 300 times.
   - A prophet had two roles:
     1. Foretelling
     2. Forthtelling[50]

WHEN DID ISAIAH TAKE PLACE? 700 B.C.

a. All prophets are usually classified as:
   - Pre-exile
   - Exile
   - Post-exile

---

[50] Wilkinson and Boa, p. 190

b. In 586 B.C., Babylon invaded Jerusalem and captured and took away many of the citizens of Jerusalem.
- Prophets who served before 586 B.C. are referred to as pre-exile.
- Prophets who served during the 70 years in Babylon, or captivity, are referred to as exile.
- Prophets who served after the 70 years of captivity are referred to as post-exile.[51]

WHERE DID ISAIAH TAKE PLACE? ISRAEL

a. Israel, northern and southern tribes

WHY WAS ISAIAH WRITTEN?

a. KEY WORD—SALVATION
- Isaiah is a mini Bible
- Isaiah 1-39 corresponds with the Old Testament
  1. Presents man's need of salvation
- Isaiah 40-66 corresponds with the New Testament
  1. Presents God's provision of salvation

b. KEY VERSE—Isaiah 6:1-8

"In the year that king Uzziah died I saw also the Lord sitting upon a throne, high and lifted up, and his train filled the temple. Above it stood the seraphim: each one had six wings; with twain he covered his face, and with twain he covered his feet,

---

[51] Rose, p. 5

and with twain he did fly. And one cried unto another, and said, Holy, holy, holy, is the LORD of hosts: the whole earth is full of his glory. And the posts of the door moved at the voice of him that cried, and the house was filled with smoke. Then said I, Woe is Me! For I am undone; because I am a man of unclean lips, and I dwell in the midst of a people of unclean lips: for mine eyes have seen the King, the LORD of hosts. Then flew one of the seraphim's unto me, having a live coal in his hand, which he had taken with the tongs from off the altar: And he laid it upon my mouth, and said, Lo, this hath touched thy lips; and thine iniquity is taken away, and thy sin purged. Also, I heard the voice of the Lord, saying, Whom shall I send, and who will go for us? Then said I, Here am I, send me."

    a. KEY TO SEE JESUS—JESUS IS THE SUFFERING SERVANT.

Chapter 22

Jeremiah 5 W's

WHO WROTE JEREMIAH? JEREMIAH

a. The son of Hilkiah, who lived two miles north of Jerusalem in Anathoth
b. "Jeremiah" means "Yahweh"
   - Throws
   - Establishes
   - Appoints[52]
   - Jeremiah was one that God appointed.

WHAT IS JEREMIAH?   MAJOR PROPHET

WHEN DID JEREMIAH TAKE PLACE? 600 B.C.[53]

---

[52] Wilkinson and Boa, p. 198
[53] Rose, p. 5

WHERE DID JEREMIAH TAKE PLACE? JUDAH

Judah in three phases:

627-605 B.C. – Judah, as Assyria and Egypt threatened

605-586 B.C. – Judah, as Babylon took over

586-580 B.C. – Jerusalem and Egypt, as Judah fell[54]

WHY WAS JEREMIAH WRITTEN?

a. KEY WORD—PROVIDENCE

God delays judgment so his people will repent

b. KEY VERSE—Jeremiah 29:11

"For I know the thoughts that I think toward you, saith the LORD, thoughts of peace, and not of evil, to give you an expected end."

c. KEY TO SEE JESUS—Jesus is the Potter with the clay in his hand.

---

[54] Wilkinson and Boa, p. 199

Chapter 23

Lamentations 5 W's

WHO WROTE LAMENTATIONS? JEREMIAH

**WHAT IS LAMENTATIONS?
MAJOR PROPHET**

a. "Lamentations" has several meanings such as "ah, how," "laments," or "tears."
b. Jeremiah was known as the weeping prophet.[1]

**WHEN DID LAMENTATIONS TAKE PLACE?
586 B.C.**

a. 586 B.C., right before the fall of Jerusalem[2]

WHERE DID LAMENTATIONS TAKE PLACE? JERUSALEM[3]

WHY WAS LAMENTATIONS WRITTEN?

a. KEY WORD—WEEPING
   - Three themes over these 5 laments:
     1. Tears over Jerusalem's fall
     2. Confession of sin from Judah
     3. Hope in God's restoration of His people
b. KEY VERSE—Lamentations 2:11
   "Mine eyes do fail with tears, my bowels are troubled, my liver is poured upon the earth, for the destruction of the daughter of my people; because the children and the sucklings swoon in the streets of the city."
c. KEY TO SEE JESUS—JESUS IS THE WEEPING PROPHET.

Notes

[1] Wilkinson and Boa, p. 207
[2] Rose, p. 5
[3] Miller, p. 205-206

Chapter 24

Ezekiel 5 W's

WHO WROTE EZEKIEL? EZEKIEL

a. Son of Buzi, who was a priest who became a prophet
b. Wife died as a sign to Judah when Nebuchadnezzar began his final siege of Jerusalem[55]

WHAT IS EZEKIEL? MAJOR PROPHET

WHEN DID EZEKIEL TAKE PLACE? 600 B.C.

a. 605-586 B.C.
b. Nebuchadnezzar destroyed Jerusalem in three stages:
   - 605 B.C. – Overcame Jehoiakim and took off key people such as Daniel
   - 597 B.C. – Carried off 10,000

---

[55] Wilkinson and Boa, p. 213

- 586 B.C. – Destroyed the city [56]

WHERE DID EZEKIEL TAKE PLACE? JERUSALEM AND BABYLON[57]

WHY WAS EZEKIEL WRITTEN?

a. KEY WORD—Restoration of Israel
   - Ezekiel, like most prophets, was written with a two-fold theme:
     1. Condemnation
     2. Consolation
b. KEY VERSE—Ezekiel 36:26-28

"A new heart also will I give you, and a new spirit will I put within you: and I will take away the stony heart out of your flesh, and I will give you an heart of flesh. And I will put my spirit within you, and cause you to walk in my statutes, and ye shall keep my judgments, and do them. And ye shall dwell in the land that I gave to your fathers; and ye shall be my people, and I will be your God."

c. KEYS SEE JESUS—
   - He is the Preacher to Dry Bones.
   - He is a Wheel in a Wheel.

---

[56] Wilkinson and Boa, p. 213-214
[57] Rose, p. 5

Chapter 25

Daniel 5 W's

WHO WROTE DANIEL? DANIEL

a. Was born of a noble Jewish family
b. "Daniel" means "God is my judge."[58]
c. Taken to Babylon and educated
d. Name changed to Belteshazzar
   - After a Babylonian god

WHAT IS DANIEL? MAJOR PROPHET

WHEN DID DANIEL TAKE PLACE? 600 B.C.

a. 600-500 B.C.[59]

---

[58] Wilkinson and Boa, p. 221
[59] Rose, p. 5

WHERE DID DANIEL TAKE PLACE? JERUSALEM AND BABYLON[60]

WHY WAS DANIEL WRITTEN?

a. KEY WORD—RESTORATION OF ISRAEL
- To encourage Jews by showing the purpose God has for Israel

b. KEY VERSE—Daniel 1:8-9

"But Daniel purposed in his heart that he would not defile himself with the portion of the king's meat, nor with the wine which he drank: therefore he requested of the prince of the eunuchs that he might not defile himself. Now God had brought Daniel into favour and tender love with the prince of the eunuchs."

c. KEY SEE JESUS—
- Jesus is the Son of Man.
- Jesus is the Fire Within Us.

---

[60] Wilkinson and Boa, p. 221

Section 5: MINOR PROPHETS

Chapter 26

Hosea 5 W's

WHO WROTE HOSEA? HOSEA

a. Hosea was the son of Beer and the husband to Gomer.
b. Hosea was also the father of two sons and a daughter. [61]
c. "Hosea" means "salvation."

WHAT IS HOSEA? MINOR PROPHET

a. Hosea ministers to the northern tribes of Israel, sometimes called Ephraim.[62]

WHEN DID HOSEA TAKE PLACE? 700 B.C.

a. The kings in Judah were Uzziah, Jothan, Ahaz, and Hezekiah.

---

[61] Wilkinson and Boa, p. 234
[62] Hanke, p. 253

b. The kings in Israel were Jeroboam II and Tiglath-Pileser.[63]

WHERE DID HOSEA TAKE PLACE? ISRAEL

a. In Israel, the northern tribes [64]

WHY WAS HOSEA WRITTEN?

a. KEY WORD—GOD'S LOVE
   - God pursues his people
b. KEY VERSE—Hosea 6:1

"Come, and let us return unto the LORD: for he hath torn, and will heal us; he hath smitten, and he will bind us up."

c. KEY TO SEE JESUS—Jesus is the Faithful Husband.

---

[63] Wilkinson and Boa, p. 234-235
[64] Rose, p. 6

Chapter 27

Joel 5 W's

WHO WROTE JOEL? JOEL

a. The son of Pethuel, meaning "persuaded of God"[65]
b. The name "Joel" means "Yahweh is God."[66]

WHAT IS JOEL? MINOR PROPHET

WHEN DID JOEL TAKE PLACE? 800 B.C.[67]

WHERE DID JOEL TAKE PLACE? JUDAH

a. Southern kingdom of Judah[68]

---

[65] Wilkinson and Boa, p. 240
[66] Hanke, p. 257
[67] Hanke, p. 257
[68] Wilkinson and Boa, p. 240-241

WHY WAS JOEL WRITTEN?

a. KEY WORD—THE DAY OF THE LORD
   - The key theme is, "The Day of the Lord."
   - Joel was written to Judah to call for them to repent.

b. KEY VERSE—Joel 2:12-13

"Therefore also now, saith the LORD, turn ye even to me with all your heart, and with fasting, and with weeping, and with mourning: And rend your heart, and not your garments, and turn unto the LORD your God: for he is gracious and merciful, slow to anger, and of great kindness, and repenteth him of the evil."

c. KEY TO SEE JESUS
   - Jesus is the Day of the Lord
   - Jesus is sending His Spirit upon His people

Chapter 28

Amos 5 W's

WHO WROTE AMOS? AMOS

WHAT IS AMOS? MINOR PROPHET

a. "Amos" is from the Hebrew meaning "to lift a burden" or "to carry," thus his name means "burden" or "burden bearer."
b. Amos lives up to his name as he lives under the burden of declaring judgement to Israel.

WHEN DID AMOS TAKE PLACE? 700 B.C.[69]

WHERE DID AMOS TAKE PLACE? ISRAEL

a. Amos was a farmer.

---

[69] Rose, p. 6

b. He does not claim to be a prophet or the son of a prophet. (Amos 7:14)
c. Amos had to leave his homeland of Judah to preach judgment to Israel.

WHY WAS AMOS WRITTEN?

a. KEY WORD—JUDGEMENT OF ISRAEL
- The key theme is the coming judgment of Israel.
b. KEY VERSE—Amos 3:2

"You only have I known of all the families of the earth: therefore I will punish you for all your iniquities."

c. KEY TO SEE JESUS—Justice

Chapter 29

Obadiah 5 W's

WHO WROTE OBADIAH? OBADIAH

a. Obadiah was an obscure prophet who lived in the southern kingdom of Judah.
b. "Obadiah" means "worshiper of Yahweh" or "servant of Yahweh."[70]

WHAT IS OBADIAH? MINOR PROPHET

WHEN DID OBADIAH TAKE PLACE? 800 B.C.[71]

WHERE DID OBADIAH TAKE PLACE? JUDAH

a. The descendants of Esau are the Edomites, which means "red" because of the red stew he traded for his birthright.

---

[70] Wilkinson and Boa, p. 251
[71] Wilkinson and Boa, p. 251

b. Genesis 27:10 says they will be cut off forever.

WHY WAS OBADIAH WRITTEN?

a. KEY WORD—JUDGEMENT OF EDOM

b. KEY VERSE—Obadiah 15

"For the day of the LORD is near upon all the heathen: as thou hast done, it shall be done unto thee: thy reward shall return upon thine own head."

c. KEY TO SEE JESUS—Jesus is the Judge.

Chapter 30

Jonah 5 W's

WHO WROTE JONAH? JONAH

a. The name "Jonah" means "dove."

WHAT IS JONAH? MINOR PROPHET

WHEN DID JONAH TAKE PLACE? 700 B.C.[72]

WHERE DID JONAH TAKE PLACE? NINEVEH[73]

Jonah wanted to go to Tarshish, God wanted him in Nineveh.

WHY WAS JONAH WRITTEN?

a. KEY WORD—REVIVAL IN NINEVEH

---

[72] Hanke, p. 268
[73] Rose, p. 6

- God calls Jonah to go preach repentance to Nineveh, but he goes the opposite direction to Tarshish.
- God gets Jonah's attention.
- He goes to Nineveh and preaches, and many are saved, but Jonah is not happy that God chose to save the city of Nineveh.

  b. KEY VERSE—Jonah 1:17

"Now the LORD had prepared a great fish to swallow up Jonah. And Jonah was in the belly of the fish three days and three nights."

  c. KEY TO SEE JESUS—Jesus is the Great Missionary.

Chapter 31

Micah 5 W's

WHO WROTE MICAH? MICAH

WHAT IS MICAH? MINOR PROPHET

WHEN DID MICAH TAKE PLACE? 700 B.C.[74]

WHERE DID MICAH TAKE PLACE? JUDAH AND ISRAEL[75]

WHY WAS MICAH WRITTEN?

a. KEY WORD—JUDGEMENT AND RESTORATION OF ISRAEL
   - Micah exposes the injustice of Judah and the righteousness of God.
b. KEY VERSE—Micah 7:7

---

[74] Rose, p. 6
[75] Rose, p. 6

"Therefore I will look unto the LORD; I will wait for the God of my salvation: my God will hear me."
  c. KEY TO SEE JESUS—Jesus casts our sin into a sea of forgetfulness.

Chapter 32

Nahum 5 W's

WHO WROTE NAHUM? NAHUM

a. A prophet in the Southern Kingdom
b. "Nahum" means "comfort" or "consolation." It is a shortened form of Nehemiah.

WHAT IS NAHUM? MINOR PROPHET

a. The destruction of the capitol city of Assyria brought hope to Israel who lived in fear that they would invade.[76]

---

[76] Wilkinson and Boa, p. 267

WHEN DID NAHUM TAKE PLACE?
600 B.C.[77]

WHERE DID NAHUM TAKE PLACE?
JUDAH AND NINEVEH[78]

WHY WAS NAHUM WRITTEN?

a. KEY WORD—JUDGMENT OF NINEVEH
- God's retribution against Nineveh but also shows the patience of God.

b. KEY VERSE—Nahum 1:7

"The LORD is good, a stronghold in the day of trouble; and He knoweth them that trust in Him."

c. KEY TO SEE JESUS
- Jesus is our future peace.

World peace –When Jesus returns and establishes His kingdom then there will be peace.

---

[77] Rose, p. 6
[78] Rose, p. 6

Chapter 33

Habakkuk 5 W's

WHO WROTE HABAKKUK? HABAKKUK

a. Proof is found in Habakkuk 1:1, 3:1.
b. Habakkuk was a prophet and may have served as a priest.
c. Habakkuk is an unusual Hebrew name derived from the verb "*habaq*" meaning "to embrace." Thus, his name means "one who embraces."
d. This is appropriate because at the end of the book he embraces God regardless of what the nation does [79]

---

[79] Hanke, p. 2739

WHAT IS HABAKKUK? MINOR PROPHET

WHEN DID HABAKKUK TAKE PLACE? 600 B.C.[80]

WHERE DID HABAKKUK TAKE PLACE? JUDAH[81]

WHY WAS HABAKKUK WRITTEN?

a. KEY WORD—FAITH
- The circumstances of life seem to contradict God's revelation of His power and purpose.

b. KEY VERSE—Habakkuk 3:19

"The LORD God is my strength, and he will make my feet like hinds' feet, and he will make me to walk upon mine high places. To the chief singer on my stringed instruments."

c. KEY TO SEE JESUS—Jesus is the crusher of injustice.

---

[80] Rose, p. 6
[81] Rose, p. 6

Chapter 34

Zephaniah 5 W's

WHO WROTE ZEPHANIAH? ZEPHANIAH

a. He may have been a descendant of King Hezekiah; and if so, he would be the only prophet of royal descent.[82]
b. "Zephaniah" means "Yahweh hides"[83]

WHAT IS ZEPHANIAH? MINOR PROPHET

WHEN DID ZEPHANIAH TAKE PLACE? 600 B.C.[84]

WHERE DID ZEPHANIAH TAKE PLACE? JUDAH

a. Judah and the nations all around Judah

---

[82] Miller, p. 275
[83] Hanke, p. 281
[84] Hanke, p. 281

WHY WAS ZEPHANIAH WRITTEN?

a. KEY WORD—JUDGMENT AND RESTORATION IN THE DAY OF THE LORD

Zephaniah 1:1-3:8 – Describes the coming day of judgment upon Judah and the nations. God will judge not only His people but the whole world. No one escapes His rule.

Zephaniah 3:9-20 – Speaks of the remnant who will survive the judgment and a time of rejoicing

b. KEY VERSE—Zephaniah 3:17

"The LORD thy God in the midst of thee is mighty; he will save, he will rejoice over thee with joy; he will rest in his love, he will joy over thee with singing."

c. KEY TO SEE JESUS—Jesus is the Warrior who saves us.

Chapter 35

Haggai 5 W's

WHO WROTE HAGGAI? HAGGAI

a. Haggai is mentioned 9 times: 1:1, 1:3, 1:12-13, 2:1, 2:10, 2:13-14, 2:20

WHAT IS HAGGAI?   MINOR PROPHET

WHEN DID HAGGAI TAKE PLACE? 500's B.C.[85]

WHERE DID HAGGAI TAKE PLACE? JUDAH[86]

WHY WAS HAGGAI WRITTEN?

a. KEY WORD—RECONSTRUCTION OF THE TEMPLE

---

[85] Rose, p. 7
[86] Rose, p. 7

- Life is rough when people put their own selfish interests before God.

b. KEY VERSE—Haggai 1:14

"And the LORD stirred up the spirit of Zerubbabel the son of Shealtiel, governor of Judah, and the spirit of Joshua the son of Josedech, the high priest, and the spirit of all the remnant of the people; and they came and did work in the house of the LORD of hosts, their God..."

c. KEY TO SEE JESUS—Jesus is the Restorer of Worship.

Chapter 36

Zechariah 5 W's

WHO WROTE ZECHARIAH? ZECHARIAH
   a. Was in the priestly line
   b. He was born in Babylon during the captivity but came to Jerusalem in the return with Zerubbabel.[87]
   c. "Zechariah" means "God remembers."

---

[87] Hanke, p. 287

WHAT IS ZECHARIAH? MINOR PROPHET

WHEN DID ZECHARIAH TAKE PLACE? 500 B.C.[88]

WHERE DID ZECHARIAH TAKE PLACE? JERUSALEM

WHY WAS ZECHARIAH WRITTEN?

    a. KEY WORD—PREPARATION OF THE MESSIAH

    b. KEY VERSE—Zechariah 1:2-3

"The LORD hath been sore displeased with your fathers. Therefore say thou unto them, Thus saith the LORD of hosts; Turn ye unto me, saith the LORD of hosts, and I will turn unto you, saith the LORD of hosts."

    c. KEY TO SEE JESUS—Jesus is our Messiah who was pierced for us.

---

[88] Rose, p. 7

Chapter 37

Malachi 5 W's

WHO WROTE MALACHI? MALACHI

a. "Malachi" means "messenger of God"[89]
b. Some think that, because Malachi means "my messenger," Malachi was not a real person, but that Ezra wrote Malachi – John Calvin believed this.
c. They use the reasoning that Malachi is the only prophet that does not mention his father's name or place of birth.
d. I stay simple and say Malachi wrote the book.

---

[89] Hanke, p. 291

The 5 W's Of Every Old Testament Book

WHAT IS MALACHI? MINOR PROPHET

WHEN DID MALACHI TAKE PLACE? 400 B.C.[90]

WHERE DID MALACHI TAKE PLACE? JUDAH[91]

WHY WAS MALACHI WRITTEN?

a. KEY WORD—RETURN
- Malachi's message was to get Israel out of disbelief, disappointment, and discouragement.[92]
-

b. KEY VERSE—Malachi 3:7
"Even from the days of your fathers ye are gone away from mine ordinances and have not kept them. Return unto me, and I will return unto you, saith the LORD of hosts. But ye said, Wherein shall we return?"

c. KEY TO SEE JESUS—Jesus is the Son who brings healing.

---

[90] Hanke, p. 291
[91] Rose, p. 7
[92] Wilkinson and Boa, p. 295

Bibliography

Biblehub.com/interlinear/exodus/1.htm

Biblehub.com/interlinear/leviticus/1.htm

Biblehub.com/interlinear/numbers/1.htm

Bible Overview. *Bible Overview*, Rose, 2004.

Galan, Benjamin. *Bible Overview*. Rose Publishing, Inc., 2012.

Hanke, Howard A., and Howard A. Hanke. *The Thompson Chain-Reference Bible Companion: a Handbook for the Classic Chain-Reference Bible*. B.B. Kirkbridge Bible Co., 1989.

Hindson, Edward E., and Elmer L. Towns. *Illustrated Bible Survey: an Introduction*. B & H Academic, 2017.

Holman Illustrated Bible Handbook. Holman Bible Publishers, 2018.

Hudson, Christopher D. *The Most Significant People, Places, and Events in the Bible: a Quickview Guide*. Zondervan, 2015.

Miller, Stephen M. *The Complete Guide to the Bible.* Barbour Books, 2015.

Ultimate Bible Guide. Holman Bible Publishers, 2016.

Wilkinson, Bruce, and Kenneth Boa. *Talk thru the Bible.* Thomas Nelson, 2005.

Willmington, H. L. *Willmington's Guide to the Bible.* Tyndale House Publishers, 2011.

ABOUT THE AUTHOR

Dr. Mike Smith,
President, Jacksonville College in Jacksonville, Texas

Dr. Smith holds several academic degrees, including an Associate of Arts from Blinn College, a Bachelor of Arts from Baylor University, and a Master of Divinity and a Master of Religious Education from Southwestern Baptist Theological Seminary in Fort Worth. He has an earned doctorate from Luther Rice Seminary, as well as a Doctor of Ministry degree and a Doctor of Philosophy degree from Southern Seminary in Louisville, Kentucky.

Dr. Smith has taught courses as Adjunct Professor at the Baptist Missionary Association Theological Seminary in Jacksonville, and for Southwestern Baptist

Theological Seminary in Fort Worth. He has served on the Jacksonville College Board of Visitors, and has also been a member of the Board of Trustees for the college.

Dr. Smith pastored churches for 17 years in Texas at Gatesville, Frost, Valley View, Edom, and Terrell. He has worked with the Home Mission Board of the Southern Baptist Convention as a church planter in Illinois, and has served as 2nd Vice Chairman of the International Mission Board for the SBC. From 1995 to 2008, Smith was Director of Missions of the Dogwood Trails Baptist Area in Jacksonville. Prior to that, he was Director of Missions at Double Mountain Baptist Area in Stamford, Texas for eight years. He served as Director of the Minister/Church Relations Department for the Southern Baptists of Texas Convention for three years before becoming president of Jacksonville College in 2011. He also teaches Old and New Testament Survey courses at Jacksonville College. He starts each class day with a devotional from Proverbs and prayer.

Mike Smith has been married to Susan Springer Smith for forty-two years. They have two children, Martha Elain Gardner and Lance Curtis Smith. They have five grandchildren, William, Emma, and Jacob Gardner, and Logan and Landon Smith. they also count as their children son-in-law, James Gardner and daughter-in-law, Ashley Smith.
His other books include:

- Conflict: Causes and Cures.
- A Proverb A Day: Daily Wisdom For Living (Available in English and Spanish)

The goal of Franklin Publishing is to enable Pastors, Evangelists, Missionaries, and Christian leaders and presenters to become published authors. Becoming a published author expands your influence and builds your ministry. You can write the book or sermon series which God has laid on your heart. We can walk that road with you.

www.FranklinPublishing.org

Come and visit our Facebook page and be sure to like and follow us to keep up with writing tips and new developments.

www.facebook.com/FranklinPublishing

www.ingramcontent.com/pod-product-compliance
Lightning Source LLC
LaVergne TN
LVHW021403080426
835508LV00020B/2436